More reviews

Division Street vibrates with the energy of immanent change, right down to the title.

David Neil Lee, author of
The Midnight Games and
Commander Zero

of *Fifty Scores*:
There is so much of the aural in our daily lives. We are enriched by noticing the detail. Here is our instruction manual.

Nelson Ball, author of *Walking*

of *Blue Mat*:
Bull's mantra, meditation and musings all poetic feels exactly like that of his long-departed Chinese partners in crime. Except they contain some of the scraps of flotsam and jetsam of our so called modern world. Bull does capture, very succinctly, our slow march against time and circumstance. It's all done carefully as mice and with admirable brevity.

Michael Dennis, author of
This Day Full of Promise

Skidmark Calligraphy: new and selected poetry
© 2023 Arthur Bull

Cover image: Arthur Bull
Cover design: Rebekah Wetmore
Editor: Andrew Wetmore

ISBN: 978-1-990187-86-5
First edition May 2023

MOOSE HOUSE
PUBLICATIONS

2475 Perotte Road
Annapolis County, NS
B0S 1A0

moosehousepress.com
info@moosehousepress.com

We live and work in Mi'kma'ki, the ancestral and unceded
territory of the Mi'kmaw People. This territory is covered
by the "Treaties of Peace and Friendship" which Mi'kmaw
and Wolastoqiyik (Maliseet) People first signed with the
British Crown in 1725. The treaties did not deal with sur-
render of lands and resources but in fact recognized
Mi'kmaq and Wolastoqiyik (Maliseet) title and estab-
lished the rules for what was to be an ongoing relation-
ship between nations. We are all Treaty people.

Also by Arthur Bull

and available from Moose House

Foreword

Here I present a selection of my poems published in books and chapbooks over the last thirty years.

To say anything insightful or interesting about this body of work is just about as hard as it would be to summarize the experience of thirty years of a life lived, with all the ebbs and flows, sudden awakenings and long periods of dormant habit, steep climbs and rapidly accelerating descents that go with it. In the end, the poems must speak for themselves.

The selection is taken from six books and seven chapbooks. (The poems from my first chapbook, *Hawthorn,* a collaboration with my late wife, Ruth, were mostly re-published in my first book, *Key to the Highway.*) Also, I did not include anything from my most recent book, a book-length poem entitled *While Looking Out at the Bay*, since it was evoked on a different scale.

In addition, the last section of this book, 'Skidmark Calligraphy', is a new series of more recent very short meditations, followed by some poems using a loose fourteener line (aka 'poulter's measure').

For some poets, making a selection like this is apparently a very difficult task, but that has not been the case for me: I simply chose the ones I like. This is a bit like having a favourite mutt that could never get a ribbon in a dog show, and probably means that some good poems have been left out because I never really warmed to them. I suppose it also means that the book itself is a kind of expressive poetic work, taken as a whole. Or that is my defence, anyway.

As with life itself, self-knowledge in poetry is elusive and hard to come by, or so I reflected as I chose these poems. There are however a couple of observations that can be made about the overall 'shape of the journey', (to borrow the phrase from Jim Harrison)—watersheds where my writing made a clear shift.

The first was a shift from books that were assorted collections of short poems without a single unifying theme, as in my first two books, to books and chapbooks that each had a single thematic focus. This started with *Fifty Scores*, a collection of prose poems as personal performance pieces, and I *Step into a World*, my chapbook about Prince Rupert BC; and continued with *Woodlot*, a meditation on the land where I live in Digby Neck, Nova Scotia, and *Blue Mat,* an homage to Chinese Song Dynasty poet Wang Yan-Li, and *Division Street*, a memoir of small town Ontario in the early 60s. This thematic approach also informed the long poem *While Looking Out at the Bay.*

The second shift was from writing free verse to writing in form. This started with sonnets (*One Hundred Sonnets),* followed by the short poems with syllabic lines in 'Skidmark Calligraphy', and loose hexameter long lines of *Looking Out at the Bay.* It is hard to explain why this shift happened, except to say that it had to do with the surprises and pleasures that come from being forced out of the habits of everyday speech by the demands of shaping words into metre and rhyme.

As well, there are undoubtedly continuities that thread through all the poems, and those I will leave for the reader to discover. There is one, however, that deserves mention, and that is my abiding attachment to classical Chinese poetry. Those long-dead, far-away writers have been my companions for more than forty years, offering me much guidance and inspiration along the way.

Looking back now, I see that, for better or worse, these poems are the result of a chronic and hard-to-explain devotion to a vocation, sparked by the life-long endeavour to—as Tennyson puts it—'follow the gleam'.

In that spirit, I humbly offer them now to you, the reader.

AB
April, 2023

For Ruth

Skidmark Calligraphy

Skidmark Calligraphy

Arthur Bull

From *Key to the Highway*

Skidmark Calligraphy

Interval

Between blackberries and deer season
the little time opens, goldenrod
laid yellow along the hillside
sprinkled with purple-stemmed asters.

When everything else has fallen away
leaving only jewelweed (or touch-me-not)
and a thistle to move together
like characters from the noh,

Unfolding their measured tension
across the platform, irruptive flocks
comb through the secret meadows
and leave us unremembered.

This is the season of the lake,
the season of smashing fruit
against the roof of the mouth,
the last berry before the cold

The hollowed place where deer have slept,
of breaking open and letting go,
when fall leans and whispers in winter's ear
let us make an interval together.

The Ming Tombs at the Royal Ontario Museum

No fall weeds overgrowing these tombs
No blossoms are settling on their stone.

Air-conditioning and broadloom:
and the curatorial skills
manage to keep away that sadness.

So far away from where they were placed,
in alignment with their `wind and water'

How could they be anything but inauspicious?
So far from the bodies they stood above.

I've been coming here since I was a kid
for the carved pleasure of their secrets,
for the dragons, the stone camels and the Buddhas

Now, I see how much time has gone by
stepping into Bloor Street and the setting sun.

Roadside Lilacs

"Lilacs always tell you that people were there."

And so if you stopped
you would find it there

Half-swallowed by purple,
a rubbled foundation,

The broken walls outline
a plan of rooms:

Kitchen, parlouar, pantry,
dining room,
back entrance.

You would stand
where the back door was
and wonder

Who stepped through it
with rabbits from the snares,

Or a mess of blackberries,
or after a time at sea.

How many welcomes
and farewells,

Skidmark Calligraphy

And what melodies heard
by the singer alone
sitting up late
on the kitchen sofa?

And outside, buried
in a wild rose thicket
a well, deep and dry,
hidden, like an eye,
trying to see
from the other world, or

Like an ear listening for
long awaited footsteps,
a voice whispering

Stay, stay.

Driving on Digby Neck, Winter Night

Dirt road frozen
to washboard waves
hardened to ridges
and solid ripples
that the car reads
like a page of braille

On the tapedeck
Charlie Patton's
grainy raspy
growl emerges
from a snowstorm
of scratches- God,

How can this life
be made so hard?
How can suffering
be made so beautiful?

Is this only
the rough surface
of events or
are they the waves
breaking the sea,
waves, feather-white,
on the Infinite
Sea of Compassion?

Bye Ya

Sometimes small animals and birds go scattering
in front of my car as though they fall
under the protection of the god Mo Shun,
deity of speed. A chipmunk's calculated

Burst, the skimming of sparrows, while
the real Monk and the real Charlie Rouse
go caroming around the car's interior
through the most improbable of changes.

We learn to travel faster than the speed of self,
the scenery glancing off the windshield: fields,
four-wheelers, farmhouses most
alive when we're running for our lives

As the chords (Trinkle Tinkle) scatter behind
as though the world for once really belongs
as much to the quick as to the dead.

The Original

How did we find ourselves here
booting it down this country road?

Radio cranked up far as it goes
pasture, the odd farm, bush, bush,

On comes *Irma* Franklin singing
Piece of My Heart- the original-

Wood sorrel, Queen Anne's lace

take it

Pastures disappear into fog

break it

Triassic jurassic the tune ends

make it

Swallowed in the flow of AM again-

You'll never find that forty-five
in a million years.

Something Almost Always Drops into Place

The shepherd asks for her hand but
she refuses but later hires him
onto her farm and the neighbouring farmer
falls in love with her but she falls
in love with the handsome sergeant
and marries him but the one he loves
dies and he leaves and so it goes

Like the changes of *Stella by Starlight*,
chord falls down to cadence,
and falling starts another sequence.

Or like when Pegasus took a plunge
behind the ridge of new maples last night.

And almost always there's a rising back
against the grain so that just when

Pandarus is about to skewer Menelaus
Homer gives us his bow- how it's made
of polished ibex horn, where he shot it,
how he fashioned it and so it goes

And holds us all there, and there
is almost always something like a ruffle
against the grain, a countervail

That suspends us against that gravity
that makes a shape for a moment and then

Is folded in and takes its place
in the joyful general collapse again.

What They Are Giving For Today

> "Spontaneity is the sign of generosity"
> —Paul-Emile Borduas

Said somewhere in
Refus Globale

Enough, more than enough
to spare: a plenitude

Rain last night
sun by midday

Inside, giving clarity
Outside, movement

Feng, The Arousing:
Lightning and thunder

Something in reserve
giving room to move around

It will be enough
to improvise.

Bailing the Boat

Each can of water I pour back in the ocean
adds up with all the rest: the sunsets, the snowy
woods, the kisses, the moments splash back in.

Higher up on the shore another
boat lies where it was hauled up,

Its still shapely planks and hull's curve
dry, splintered, paint-pealed, intact-
'Comes a time when they just won't float'

And further up in the grass and alders,
another, ribs opened, deck and cabin
flat as a losing poker hand.

Moments do not seem to gather here,
and one unaccumulated life
unravels as fast as it can knit.

The flood tide, drawing back into itself, the waves
lapping and overlapping, of a light surf, mesh
with the sweet splash of water entering water.

Skidmark Calligraphy

Arthur Bull

From *The Lake Diary*

Skidmark Calligraphy

Lake Diary

i)
This morning the lake
said take this, the shock
that the coming and the going
happen at just about
the same time.

That the first thing
 dawn does is pour pink
over the whole surface.

That the last thing
the coyotes do before they sleep
is let out one
final fading round of predatory song.

The hurry out to the middle,
the scattering of startled
ducks from the reeds,
how they spread out,
a single arpeggio

ii)
That accompanies the easy
undoing of night,
night the singular,

Skidmark Calligraphy

shadows fading
fast as dreams,
absorbed multicoloured
leaves emerging
doubled along the shore.

The canoe scrapes on rocks,
(lake's low, drought season)
scratching off green paint,
finding red beneath,
the parting of the lily

Pads, going in, going in,
the yellowing of each
lily into daylight
(paddling faster now)
the lifting of each layer,
deeper so

iii)
What never happens is completion.
The lake receives dawn only so far,
receives the paddle's scar
a split second,
losing night. The invisibility

Of coyotes, absorbed now
in a shadow world, sabotaged by sunlight,
broken ladder of sentences,
and unrelenting streams that pour

like little Amazons
into the rippling heart,

Like hours, exhausted
finally going off to sleep with one last cry,
into the hurt centre,
the paddle drawing through sunlight's shreds.

Take this, it says, this is goodbye.

iv)
This morning the lake,
pockmarked by raindrops,
gets rhythm

Each ring cut
by the rings around it,
each one says

Drop. Ripple. Break.
Then go. (Unspoken)
How much

Can you miss someone?
Shadow stripes
stones, olive-grey

On the lake bed
below. (Unheard)
I didn't know.

Skidmark Calligraphy

v)
This morning the lake
was just barely touched

by a downhanging maple,
already red

that cooled its reflection
in a deeper blue.

I took those colours,
renaming them

vermilion and cobalt,
to dress my sorrow in.

vi)
This morning the lake
took away my hat.
Across the front
it said *Amistad
Freedom*. I lost it
on a perfectly calm
day on the lake-
no wind, nothing,
no reason, nothing
that I could see.
When I stepped
into the canoe

I had it on and
when I got out.
my hat was gone.
The hat that said
Amistad Freedom
across the front.

vii)
After Su Shi

This morning the lake
was edged with fast
flying black clouds
like ink, not quite
covering the hills,
and big white raindrops
splashed on the canoe
like bouncing pearls.
In a flicker
a sudden wind
swept away the storm
and all at once
there was the sky
in the lake again

viii)
This morning the lake
was all sunlight
flaring across, all
glitter and motion

Skidmark Calligraphy

in a seam of mica.
I paddled into it,
blinded, not knowing
which shore
I was coming to
until I heard
through over-
hanging boughs
Charlie Parker
reciting a sutra
into that light,
a tune previously
known as
Embraceable You,
or else it was
a song sparrow.

ix)
This morning the lake
 held three white balloons
that had broken free
apparently
from a children's
birthday party
in the picnic park
across the lake.
They floated over
then got caught
on a hawthorn branch.
However they looked

to a six-year-old
as they drifting away,
they now appear
to me to be perfect,
perfect and perfectly
temporary.

x)
After Ou Yangxiu

This morning the lake
was so windless
no line marked it
except the ripples
that gathered round
my paddle and moved
outwards to the shore
to send ducks
thrashing up the bank,
and except for their shadows
ribboning along
the sandy bottom.
And everything was silent
under sky's mother-of pearl,
except the bow's
shearing through
the tall water reeds.
And nothing disturbed
the air held by the heat
except by a little trout

Skidmark Calligraphy

that splashed in the shallows.
And nobody spoke
except for the lake
itself, saying:
This is heaven,
this is earth.

xi)
After Ouyang Xiu

This morning the lake
so smooth and calm
caught me off guard
reminding me
of your words from
across wide oceans
and over long ages:

Green on the north shore
green on the south shore

Who knows the grief
 of final parting?

My face stained with tears
your face stained with tears

We dreamed in vain
 of our futures together

But the now the sun
no longer rises.

xii)
This morning the lake
wrote a treatise
on stability and change.
Shreds of clouds
steamed across the sky.
Out-of-nowhere winds
started strumming
a choppy pattern
across the surface.
I turned the canoe
into the wind
and paddled harder.
I couldn't see bottom:
there were too many waves
and I was too busy
to look down anyway.

xiii)
This morning the lake
was raked by a wind
that said winter's coming
so I went over there
to get the canoe
and bring it home.
A short portage
with the weight balanced

Skidmark Calligraphy

that I make every year
at about this time.
When I came to that place
where I keep it hid
back up in the woods
behind some alders,
the canoe was gone.
Stolen by somebody.
After waiting the time
it took to understand
what had happened there
I walked back home,
round the lake again
and along the road
for that one last time.

xiv)
Coda
Zhuangzi VI.4-5

You hide your boat in a ravine
or in a swamp
thinking to yourself
it will be safe.
But in the night
someone comes,
someone strong enough
to lift it up
and carry it off
and in your darkness

you'd never know
what had happened.
Something large seems
like a perfect place
to hide something small in,
but that something
can vanish into
something else.
Only by hiding
everything in everything
so there's nothing
more to vanish into,
only then do you reach
into the vast and timeless
       nature of things.

Major Thirds

Flying home,
what I left
unsaid saddens me.

The seatbelt sign,
the little chime
with its two notes

In major thirds,
repeated so
the kid ahead

Picks up on them,
and mimicking,
chimes in too.

His little voice
(boo-doo, boo-doo)
keeps on until

From somewhere
it comes to me
where these notes are from:

The opening of Ellington's
Creole Love Call,
the gentle clarinet

Arthur Bull

Trio laying down
a soft bed
for the wordless

Vocal. Funny how
regret can begin
to get so familiar,

Sound so sweet
And mournful. Clouds
full to bursting

Their whites
Give over to blue,
And then to grey.

We enter them,
the little hand
on the seat back,

And the major thirds,
lifting, leaving,
forgetting to cry.

The Golden City

The only restaurant open at 4 am.
GOLDEN CITY CHINESE AND CANADIAN FOOD.
You ordered in Cantonese,
       I drank scotch from a teacup.

Someone once said you were flighty
I still wonder what that would mean.

Gamblers and detectives, a few cabbies,
nursing their wins and losses in secret worlds,
unreadable to me, all around us and distant

Like quotes on the lacquer trimmed banners-
maybe Confucius holding up his finger saying

I will not worry about being known by others
but I will worry about not knowing them
or hard-boiled Chuang Tzu, with a laugh:

There is a limit to life, but there is no limit
to knowledge. To pursue what is unlimited
       with what is limited

Is a dangerous thing. Thirty years ago:
you and I in the Golden City, how far away is that?
There and not there, here and not here, what
difference now?

The Silver Dollar

After he killed King
James Earl Ray
came here for a drink.

Upstairs, the organ trio
and strippers: The Lounge.

Downstairs, beer.
Where everybody's from
is places like Red Lake,
Rice Lake, Sandy Lake,
Grassy Narrows, Oneida,
Kapuskasing. Batchewana.
Dancin' and drinkin'.

In the men's washroom
I noticed a hole in the wall
where a fist had gone through
the plaster and cracked the plywood

The band upstairs
swung into *Out of Nowhere*

Skidmark Calligraphy

And I thought of a hand
going into clear water
after a shiny object,
the refracted arm
going right through
a face's reflection,

And I thought then that
I don't know anything
I don't know anything at all
I don't know anything at all about this world.

Attention Shoppers

What you can find in a supermarket:
A Charlie Christian solo embedded
In a Benny Goodman tune, embedded
in the muzak.The *I Ching* supposedly
composed by a King Wen
in the 12th Century BC
between a diet book and
How to Talk to Your Cat.
A small purple bottled stopper
somehow mixed up with your change.
We are all archeologists here,
wheeling our shopping carts
We are all piecing together the shards.
And out in the parking lot
Immersed in a sea of vehicles,
a woman is picking rosehips from
a bush in a concrete box.
To no one particular she says,
"Good for tea, you know, good for colds"

Skidmark Calligraphy

Arthur Bull

From *Fifty Scores*

Skidmark Calligraphy

Arrange a selection of pieces of driftwood in a line on a soft bed of plant life (moss, lichen, sea grass). Work your way along it, back and forth, until you have found a melody and rhythm. Factor in the movement of your body. Factor in the movement of the sea.

When splitting cordwood, punctuate the single crack of your ax with the marimba trill of each split piece, as it falls on the pile of split pieces. (Each piece's particular tone ornaments the sameness of the axe's force.)

The next time you are flying put on the ear phones and turn the channel dial as fast as you can with one hand, while alternating between "+" and "-" on the volume dial with the other hand, until you find a regular pulse with which to accompany the clouds

(After John Oswald)

When doing the dishes, orchestrate and arrange sections by timbre: cutlery, dishes, pots, water, and your voice humming. Add a coda of the water draining.

Skidmark Calligraphy

On a windy day, stand by a brook in the woods near the ocean. Move your attention from foreground (brook) to middle ground (branch-wind cracking-soughing) to the background (surf), before gradually letting the usual small sounds of the forest break in.

Some evening, find a pond or a bog filled with singing frogs. Approach, noting how the peepers get quieter as you get nearer, until there are only trios, duets or solos. Walk away until the full chorus resumes. Repeat several times, until you and they have established a macro-rhythmic form of a piece.

(After Verdi)

Find an echo in a valley or against a building, and test it, measuring the interval with the loudest, shortest wordless sound your voice can make. Yell once, twice, three times, four times, as far as you can go and still get back to its complete echo.

(After James Brown)

Make a traditional quilt the score of a percussion piece, and give each patch a (drum, hand clap, bell, word) sound, following the regularities and deviances of the pattern.

One autumn, find a place with lots of fallen leaves and walk through them, kicking up a swishing rhythm with your feet. Find two sticks and strike them together, occasionally in between the "ride cymbal" beats.

(After Jo Jones)

While chopping vegetables like carrots or parsnips, attend to the "sshh" of the knife going through with the "kkk" as it hits the cutting board, arranging the rhythm and tempo to the sound of oil heating in the wok.

Hook a rubber band across your lower teeth, and stretch it out with three fingers on each hand, plucking with your forefingers. Change the tuning by spreading your fingers and your jaw.
(After Moroccan street musicians)

String a hundred feet of wire from tree to tree in a wilderness area, and connect it to a high impedance input of an audio amplifier. Play duets with tweaks, bonks and whistles produced by distant lightning or by sunspots, or just dance.

Skidmark Calligraphy

Take out all the pot lids in your kitchen, and find their character by striking each with a wooden spoon, then holding the pot lid to your ear. Continue until you have established a cycle. Let the tempo be determined by how long it takes to pick up and put down the pot lids, and by the length of each one's rings.

The next time someone leaves you, slamming the door behind them, allow that sound to echo amongst your thoughts and feelings, and having found the pulse of that echo, make up a short melody to go with it.

(After Son House)

Hold the skeleton of a fish against your skull, just behind your ear, and pluck the ribs, like a harp, while humming the first melody you can remember hearing.

Like a child, blow on a blade of grass stretched between fingers and palms, and pressed together. Hold the notes as long as possible, as you walk across a field, and note how the blade's tune follows the contours of the field, and the rhythm of your life.

Answer the song of an owl with first two notes of
"Stella by Starlight"; accompany the dial tone of your
telephone with the first two notes of "Misty."

In an undefined wash of sound—the ocean, traffic,
air-conditioning—find the pitch, timbre and volume
bandwidth it masks. Make sounds—bells,
harmonica, voice—that emerge from it, then
disappear into it, like boats in the fog.

The next time you're canoeing, listen to the music
the paddle makes. Entry, sweepback, exit, drip. Vary
tempo with changing strokes, jay to draw, feather to
duffek, brace to off-side, and so forth. Alternate with
extended sequences of silent gliding.

While brushing your teeth, modify the oral cavity
sound rhythmically as you brush over the molars in
a counter rhythm, giving the wakawaka of a wah-
wah guitar. Accompany with deep chest sound funk
bass line.

(After George Clinton)

Throw a plate in the air and before it reaches the
floor—while it hangs suspended for what could be a
long time, in the relative awareness of that moment
—take a deep breath and sing a single note.

Skidmark Calligraphy

Memorize a translation of "Drinking Under the Moon" by Li Po. Pour two glasses of wine. Alternate reciting the lines of the poem, swallows of wine, and faint ringing on of the glass you are drinking from, noting the descending sequence of tones as it empties. Keep the other glass full, for the moon.

Take a small instrument—flute, pennywhistle, harmonica—to a busy construction site, and play along.

During a light rain, stand in the woods in a place with many kinds of flat-leaved plants and trees and, out of the cloud of sound particles, start to hear the raindrops' varied pitches and rhythms, and how their slowly emerging sequences and clusters clench and release into the wet air.

(After Xennakis)

Pee into a brook. Hear the tiny bells of the splash as it joins the dancer's ankle bells of the brook's rippling.

Taking apart a barn or some other old building with a crowbar, listen to the parting wood music: Take the music—a donkey's braying, a sailing ship in a high wind, or Albert Ayler's saxophone—as a long whining, groaning counter-melody to your work. Imagine all the embedded sounds of life and death that are being released as the barn comes apart.

Have someone kiss you on the ear three times; listen (don't speak) to the merging of your breath and the kissing sound. Repeat, replacing the third kiss with his or her tongue touching the inside of your ear.

While undressing someone else, follow the sequence of clothing music: Velcro, snaps, zippers. This also works as a duet.

Go to a place where great suffering has happened—a battle, an expulsion, a massacre—and make up a song of acknowledgement.

From the shore of a lake skip a stone, and sing one note for each glance it makes. While you are looking for the next smooth stone, think up another short melody.

Skidmark Calligraphy

Kick the gravel as you walk along a driveway so that it sounds like the scratchy static of an old 78, singing "When You've Got a Good Friend" by Robert Johnson.

Turn on all the buzzers, timers. digital alarms, and other beepers in your house; then walk from room to room, drumming.

At the beginning of a walk in the woods, break off a stick to bring along. As you go, listen to the rhythm of your breath, the rhythm of your footstep and the cross-rhythms of both together. When you can hear where they touch and part, then start tapping there, on the trees you pass, bringing each tree's unique voice into the chorus.

Sing a duet with a baby.

At the laundromat, get the rhythm of one washer, then gradually add the cross-rhythms of the others, one by one, until you can have the whole ensemble, then hum a melody line, which you can keep going with variations into the send movement (the dryer), and *a cappella*, when you fold the clothes.

Listen to the music locked in all things.

From *Woodlot*

Skidmark Calligraphy

Lit up, light green, lichen-covered
rock pile in a clearing, settlers' work,
shaft of sunlight, made luminous

Those days of work, stone by stone
dug up, hauled, piled sweating
torsos, oxen groaning under the yoke

What hardship bought: nothing.
What was yours was not
Yours. What is mine is not mine.

When a new owner walks this land
a hundred years from now
what thought will he know of me?

Sun withdraws, stones
submerge in a pool of shadow.

Skidmark Calligraphy

Low mossy stone walls
        between what and what,
separate nothing

From nothing. Their meaning
      collapsed now, dotted
      with mayflowers and fade

Into dusk, property
      lines now softly erased

Where there are no walls
      there will be no fear
          so said Sariputra

Arthur Bull

A scraggly spruce
clinging for dear life
to a solitary
basalt boulder.

Deep in the woods.
no soil to hold
onto there except
a layer of lichen.

Clinging to life,
until last night
a gale tipped it
over like a lid,

Exposing the fine
capillaries, the whole
of its nervous system
of roots to the air,

Lying sideways
detached but not up-
rooted because it
never was rooted.

Skidmark Calligraphy

[Bark beetle dead spruce]

The soil here is so shallow
 a thin carpet of earth
on a basalt floor. No surprise

That trees can't hold, that they
rise dead and white into the air
floating heavenwards, choir gowns

Flapping in the breeze, voices
Raised with their favourite hymns

Rock maple branches
    reach into the pasture
        beseeching sunlight

Held upward
    the suppliants gnarled arms
        clasping the knees of life

As sacred heaven longs
    to pierce the earth, so love
        takes hold of earth to join in marriage

[Sophocles, *The Suppliants,* trans. ab]

Skidmark Calligraphy

Zhuangzi said when great nature sighs
we hear the winds, noiseless in themselves,
awakening voices from other beings, blowing

From every opening sounding loud voices
through every boll, snout socket, crotch
Groove, joint, cranny, hollow

You hear bawling, roaring, whistling, cracking
shouting, banging, grumblings,deep droning,
sad flutes, each voice conversing with the other

And when the wind dies down, the openings
empty out their last sound, have you heard
how everything then trembles and subsides?

Yu replied: I understand:The music of earth sings
 through a thousand holes, human music is played
 on flutes and horns, and we ask ourselves

 What then makes the music of heaven?

Zhuangzi (ii. I.]

Up in the upper
pasture now
crowded with alders
The rusted
old harrow
plaited tight
to the ground
by bindweed:

The landholder
is now held
by the land

Skidmark Calligraphy

Whatever flowers and fruits there are, and whatever kinds of medicine, and whatever jewels exist in this world, and whatever clean refreshing waters;

Likewise moss-covered gullies, forest groves, quiet and joyful places, heavenly trees dripping with pale green old man's beard, branches laden with scarlet chokecherries;

The cluster of red trilliums appearing only briefly through the woody mat, the mossy basalt boulders solitary deep in the woods

Fragrances of the celestial realms, balsam incense, wishing trees and jewel trees, uncultivated harvests, and all ornaments that are worthy to be offered;

Sloughs and bogs thick with wild roses, and the beautiful cry of wild geese, the beating of the grouse's wings in the alders, everything unowned within the limitless spheres of space.

Creating these things in my mind, I offer them to the supreme ones as well as their children: 0 Compassionate Ones, think kindly of me and accept these offerings of mine.

[After Shantideva, Bodhisattvacharyavatara, Chapt. II]

I call on you, coves and headlands,
And you, animals who have shared my paths.
I call on you and have no one else to call

I never was meant to leave you in the end
and you shall be with me at my death

[Sophocles *Philoctetes*]

Skidmark Calligraphy

Arthur Bull

From *Blue Mat – poems after Yang Wanli*

Skidmark Calligraphy

Blue Mat

I am joined on my blue rubber yoga mat
by a slug, moving as though all its senses
were concentrated in two fleshy horns,
their round nubs stressing and straining
to extend perception to the whole universe:
seems pretty confident of getting it right.
I close my eyes awhile, then open them:
the slug is gone, having left behind only
a crooked white trail, shapely, still wet.

Barn

Over twenty years
Angus's barn first leaned,
then went on its knees,
then fell and lay there
quietly on its side
for a while until
flattened out, almost
disappeared except
for the pile of stones
its foundation became
and this was long after
Angus himself had gone,
not quite forgotten
but leaving no sign.

Taking the Dawn Ferry
Yang Wanli

Can't see
river and mountain
beyond the fog

Only pig and chicken
noises tell me
there's a village there

The frost has laid
deep as snow
on the ferry deck

Fly

I noticed
a housefly
warming itself
on the windowsill
rubbing its legs
together and
enjoying
the sunshine
then seeming
to know just
when the light
was about
to shift to
move over
to the next
windowsill.

Yan Wanli (Trans. ab)

Every summer our neighbours grew a pig,
treated it very well, the kids even
named it, the most recent being Zorro.
They would visit him and scratch his forehead
with a stick, which he enjoyed immensely
unaware that this was to make him calm
when the time came to scratch his forehead
with the barrel of a hunting rifle.

Skidmark Calligraphy

A wooden footbridge
                 reflected in the river's
                     polished mahogany

Hundreds of wild geese
                 dot the bay
                     like spilled ink

At the first sound
                 of my footfall
                     on the planks

They rise, and their startled
                 cries fill the morning
                     with characters.

Arthur Bull

I visited the ancient terrace
above the tops of banyan trees

The ocean far below, dark
as wine in a jade cup

Once, the King of Yueh sang
and danced in the spring wind here.

Today there is only the spring wind.

Skidmark Calligraphy

River clear and calm
heavy rain in the gorge

Midnight: cold splashing
of raindrops, ten thousand

Pearls clattering
on a glass plate

Goes right to the bone

I wake from the dream
scratch my head, listen

and listen until the sunrise

All my life I've heard rain
Now, I am an old man

I understand something
for the very first time:

the sound of rain at night.

Vancouver 1970

Along with the joint,
you passed a matchbook
you'd written on
"Shadows of returning
geese go by".
You had expected
me to write
the next line, but
I was too frozen
with self-doubt
to see your invite.
Now I don't know
where you are or even
if you are still alive,
the first real poet
I ever met, many,
many years ago.
Today I remember
you and write the line:
'The flare of a match
struck in the darkness'

Mountain Journey (1)

The late Song poet Fan Changda, a friend of Yang Wanli, wrote an essay describing a visit to Emei Shan in Szechuan Province. In it he describes his experience of the Buddha Light, a phenomenon that is said to occur when watching the dawn at the summit of the mountain. The following is account of a visit to Emei Shan by my partner and me in 2002. Emei Shan is one of the five Buddhist Sacred Mountains of China.

After arriving at the foot of the mountain by bus from Chengdu, we booked into the Teddy Bear Inn and my partner decided to rest since she was not feeling well.

I went wandering around the foot of the mountain, enjoying the lush semitropical vegetation, red carved calligraphy in the rock and stalls selling herbal teas and medicines form the mountain. I eventually came to a stream and decided to make a video that was in keeping with the peaceful feeling of this place. Looking at it now, there's nothing about it that is unique to Emai Shan—it could be any stream anywhere. It is also ruined by being poorly shot: the camera jumps around, following a tiny brilliantly coloured bird perched a rock in the stream, and then trying to follow it as it hopped away to another rock. Far from being calm and meditative, the video ends up being jerky and unfocused.

Later we made our way part way up the mountain and stayed in a Buddhist convent. A nun asked us if we wanted to be wakened attend the morning prayers, which we agreed to. At 4:30 am we stumbled down half asleep into the temple's main hall, where we heard sutras chanted in unison by nuns as they walked around the room, punctuated by the sound of huge bells and drums. Later, we the joined them excellent breakfast of rice porridge, raw ginger, peanuts and pickled greens.

From there we took a cable car to the summit where we stayed overnight so that we could see the dawn, and perhaps even the Buddha Light. Because it was so much colder up there and people were not prepared, the inn loaned everyone huge People's Liberation Army greatcoats to wear as went to see the sunrise. We didn't see the Buddha Light as it turned out, but we did see the sun appear dramatically from below the clouds. Several dozen others, all Chinese, also stood at the railing watching in silence for what seemed like a long time. The man beside me said under his breath 'Hen piaoliang a' (so beautiful).

Many great poems have been written about Emei Shan. Perhaps the most famous is by Li Bai, which I had translated twenty years ago.

On Hearing the Lute Playing of a Monk from Shu

The monk from Shu, carrying his silk instrument bag,
Was coming down the western slope of Emei
Mountain.

His hand ran over the strings for me:
the windsound of pine in a thousand valleys.

A flowing stream cleanses the traveller's heart,
An harmonic dying amongst frozen bells.

I didn't feel evening enter those green hills
Or the darkening layers of autumn clouds.

Li Bai (translated AB)

Mountain Journey (2)
Wutai Shan

Wutai Shan, in Shanxi Province, is also one of the four Buddhist Sacred Mountains of China. Wŭtái is the home of the Bodhisattva of wisdom, Mañjuśrī or Wénshū (文殊) in Chinese.

Our journey to Wutai Shan began in Datong where we boarded a very rickety buss, packed with pilgrims, as well as several monks and nuns. After about an hour we started to ascend a narrow two-lane road that clung to the side of a mountain with a steep and distant drop on our left. We soon found ourselves, much to our surprise in the middle of simple gridlock traffic jam of coal trucks going to a coal mine up in the mountains. Every once in a while the driver would pull out into the oncoming lane and race past half a dozen trucks, hoping that there would be a gap in the line where he could pull in, and that there would be no oncoming trucks. This went on for several hours, and then it began to snow, at first it just a dusting, hardy noticeable, but soon becoming much heavier, until we all realized that we were in the middle of a major blizzard. Having got past the truck traffic jam, the bus was now sliding and skidding all over the road and had to slow down to crawl. After awhile it became evident that we were running out of gas, and the driver was forced to turn off the heat to conserve fuel. Apparently rethinking the route completely, he then took another road that led downward and then up again, through an area that seemed to be less snowy. We stopped at a roadside café in mountain village, where the driver and the tout went in for a break. (What I call the tout is a person who is universally present in most countries in the world where there are small privately run bus services. Their job is to hang out the door and yell the destinations to people along the roadside.) When they came back they had an almost emptied a big bottle of baijiu ('white lightning' by any other name) and were completely drunk. By this time no one seemed to care at all. We finally arrived in the village of Wutai Shan, after nineteen hours.

II
When we awoke the next morning, we found ourselves in a brilliantly lit snowy village with many temples and stupas both in the town and on the hilltops surrounding the plateau. The atmosphere was relaxed and friendly, and there were few tourists, possibly because this was the off-season for pilgrimages. We had heard that in the summer it is like crowded medieval fair all summer. We walked up to one of the temples and found ourselves in an atmosphere of friendly welcome by nuns and monks. There was sweetness and evenness in the clear mountain air.

III

After a very enjoyable stay of a few days we decided to descend the mountain to Taiyuan., the next city to the south. Again, it was a rickety bus, also very full, but this time it was as sunny, without a cloud din the sky. Maybe because there was nothing terrifying, the noise of the old bus shaking an creaking much louder, so I plugged in my earphones and listed to a tape. After a few minutes, I noticed the tout waving at me and pointing to my Walkman. After a confusing exchange involving many hand gestures, I realized he wanted me to give him the cassette I was listening so he could put it in the bus's cassette deck so everyone could hear it. Thus it was that we descended Wutai Shan, with a bus full of Buddhist pilgrims, monks and nuns nodding and tapping their feet to the sound of Howlin' Wolf.

Skidmark Calligraphy

Arthur Bull

From *Division Street*

Skidmark Calligraphy

School

I
Everything we learned was contained in lists:
La Vérendrye, Champlain, Mackenzie, Thompson,
Fraser, Cabot, Frobisher, Cartier,
Northumberland, Dufferin, Lennox, Haldimand,
Brant, Middlesex, Simcoe, Frontenac,
stamen, pistil, petal, filament,
sepal, St. Lawrence, Mackenzie, Fraser,
Athabaska, head, thorax, abdomen.
Speed was more important than knowledge,
racing through timetables and spelling bees,
litanies rhymed off, carried with breathless
rapidity, as though there would come a time
in our lives when we'd find we had nothing
but names, and names alone could save us.

II
Our reader was called *High Flight*,
with all the usual anthology pieces
(poems by Maesfield, Frost, Houseman)
 as well as some Canadian pieces:

A poem by Wilfred Campbell
that stated 'the hour before the flush of dawn'
[laughing behind our hands]

Skidmark Calligraphy

And one by Duncan Campbell Scott
with the line 'The hawks fell twanging from the sky'
[like Duane Eddy's guitar?]

An essay by Vincent Massey
on being a Canadian:
'touch of breeziness and an alertness
that suggest the new world'
[really???]

It had colour plates of paintings
by the Group of Seven:

The Red Maple by AY Jackson
[daydreaming: *looking through black tree
branches into a world of red leaves fluttering
over churning rapids]*

Northern River by Tom Thompson
[daydreaming: *mesh of branches,: distant touch
of colour reflected on river , bending far away]*

One section called 'Growing Up In Canada '
began with a drawing of a young man
attempting to scale a sheer vertical rock face
in the middle of a barren treeless wilderness
[Yes, that sounded about right].

Some Things We Didn't Know

That smoking is bad for you. In fact we went from
stronger to stronger brands: Black Cat, Sweet
Caporal, Export A and finally Old Port Cigarillos,
even though they made us sick. Once we even
smoked punk wood that we found growing near the
lake.

That X-rays are dangerous. We used to stop at the
shoe store on the way home at lunchtime to put our
feet in the x-ray machine and look at our feet bones,
and once I had a Planter's Wart that was removed by
a huge x-ray gun operated by a man in a lead suit.
The wart fell off within a day.

That the CIA had murdered Patrice Lumumba,
President of the Democratic Republic of Congo.

That some children in our classrooms were often
seriously harmed by their own parents

That the last Lake Ontario salmon was caught in
1898, after which they became extinct.

That the RCAF firebombed Hamburg and Dresden.

That Duncan Campbell Scott, whose poem beginning
with the line 'Last night a storm fell on the world'

was in our reader, was also the Deputy Minister of the Department of Indian Affairs, and the main architect of the residential schools policy.

That some kids in our class were being taken away from their families by the government, and sent to residential schools.

That we were in someone else's place, and that their descendants were among our classmates.

Softball

Saturday summer evenings,
we'd go down to the lake
to watch the girls' softball.
The games were long and relaxed,
slow-paced, almost languorous.
We went to watch the pitchers,
each one with her own unique style:
the baroque wind-up, the eccentric
underhand turn and release
with a curlicue twist, the knee dip
then slightest shake of the head.
Through the heat and murmur
of conversation the occasional
cheer or jeer from the stands.
From the Pav, music on the PA
warming up for the dance later
drifted across the vague wash
of surf through the summer night:
the sound of the Shirelles singing
I've been told when a boy kiss a girl,
take a trip around the world.

Spacemaster X-7

I
A space probe returns to earth covered
with a mysterious fungus that transforms
into an ever-growing pile of space rust
that, when accidentally tinged with human blood,
became Bloodrust, threatening to cover the earth.

II
The idea of uncontrollably toxic
substances was quite familiar to us.
How Factory Creek flowed bright orange
from the General Wire and Cable Company,
and the mountains of emerald green
algae blooms, larded with of dead smelts,
so thick they slowed the waves.

III
In front the General Foods plant (Cobourg's biggest
a thriving product of Ontario's
            branchplant economy)
they had a huge sign that said GENERAL FOODS
HOME OF JELL-O, hence known as *The Jell-O Factory*.
For us, it was important
            for another reason altogether:
in each box of *Jell-O* they put a free hockey coin,
a little plastic disc holding a photo of an NHL player
like a Russian icon, they were all there: Sawchuk,

Mahovolich, Howe, Keon, Baun, Shack, Bower, Hull
Geoffrion, Belliveau, Lafleur and the Rocket.
For a time, they were the main schoolyard currency.
So it was a huge discovery
      to learn that General Foods
was dumping massive amounts of unsold *Jell-O*
in the woods behind the plant,
      including hockey coins.
When we got there,
      we found that the boxes had mostly
been dissolved by rain leaving a huge mountain
of pastel coloured sludge that we waded through
in rubber boots, picking out
      the coins by the hundreds.

IV
When we hiked to Port Hope we'd pass
Eldorado Mining and Refining,
where they refined the uranium
for the Manhattan Project, and all
the early atomic bombs, and buried,
some say, half a million cubic metres
of radioactive waste around the town
in parks, fields, ravines, the harbour
and even in the material that people
used to build their houses with.
We had no idea how close we were
to history which, like radiation,
is everywhere, and always invisible.

Ambrose

As a little kid I had an extreme fear of dogs
And, for some reason (this was probably why),
I was given the job of looking after the new dog,
a bulldog named Ambrose, (after the saint).
To say Ambrose was flawed would be serious
understatement. He was a dog afflicted
with multiple diseases and bad habits
all of which he carried like a badge of honour.
Infected ears, running fluids, a 'double eyelid'
that made a white bubble under one eye,
farting and drooling without pause,
able to leg-fuck at a moment's notice,
so ugly that once some American tourists
stopped their car to tell me that I should
put such a dangerous animal on a leash.
He was the perfect expression of the shock
 and wonderment of embodiment itself,
and was everything I could want in a dog.
Once, when we were painting the garage
green, one of my friends dabbed the paintbrush
on his balls creating a spectacle both indelible
and unmentionable that he happily
presented to the Ladies Auxiliary tea
and other church-related gatherings.

Politics

Politics, another bizarre preoccupation
of adults, would make its appearance
from time to time in the life of the town.
Dief came during an election campaign
to made a speech at the Pav. As he left,
I shook his hand, and remember wondering
how someone that profoundly unattractive
could be the Prime Minister of Canada.
Sometimes there were election rallies
that they would pack with school kids.
Once we were sent by bus to Kingston
to hear Pearson speak in the hockey arena.
Suddenly, right in middle of his speech,
a crowd of Tories, who'd been strategically
positioned around the stage, pulled out
their signs, started waving them and yelling
slogans, until they were strong-armed outside.
Politics was very similar to the carnie
that came about once a year every summer:
the freak show, the girlie show, dodgy rides,
cotton candy and many kinds of toss games
with prizes of giant pink stuffed animals.

Port Hope Drive-In

I
If you go straight north of the Drive-In
first you cross fields of reddish dirt
ploughed by tiny tractors trailing plumes
of dust-drawn parallels in the distance,
then over eskers and drumlins shaped
by a recent glacier's slow hand turning
like a potter's, rolling side to side,
dragging its body's leisurely retreat,
then over Rice Lake named for wild rice
sustainer of life, called *manoomin* (not
rice at all) then to the Serpent Mounds,
the winding hills that hold of the bones
who sing this place's future and its past.

II
At the Drive-In, what's showing is
        The Siege of Syracuse
Italian sword-and-sandals about the Roman invasion
of Sicily in 214 BC. It includes
        the story of Archimedes
who was working for the King of Sicily at the time
of the Roman conquest, that very same Archimedes
inventor of the heat ray, the screw pump,
        the giant claw,
who discovered many geometrical theorems

including
how to find the surface area and volume of a sphere,
the volume of an irregular shaped object and, most
beautifully, how you get the area of a circle
      (multiplying π times the square of it radius).
That same Archimedes
was inscribing diagrams in the dust in his courtyard
when Roman soldiers entered and
      ordered him to come
and report to the victorious Roman general
      Marcellus,
to which he replied, it is said:
      "Do not disturb my circles",
for which he was murdered, right then and there.

The Cold War

I
During the Cuban Missile Crisis
a girl ran home at recess in tears.
Adults were talking to children
about the very real possibility
of *everyone* being burned alive.
We took this all in our stride,
since we'd seen the great Kaiju
monster movies at the Park.
We knew what would happen,
the way crowds would flee
looking over their shoulders,
as they ran toward the camera,
the wind from Mothra's wings
collapsing bridges and buildings,
Godzilla advancing, unstoppable,
through smoke of burning cities
(himself the result of nuclear war)
and how the world was fragile,
crafted, meticulous and delicate,
of rice paper, string and cardboard.

Empire

You were caught between two empires-
one fading and one coming on strong.
Our spellers said *aeroplane* and *programme*,
we pledged allegiance to the British Empire
every morning and pink areas on the roll-up
map of the world that told us how once
we had belonged to some exotic empire
an imperial dream, now dusty and tattered.
When the Queen came we sat on the curb
In flannel shorts with little union Jacks
knowing something had already gone past.
At the same time we sensed the Americans
were closing in on us from every direction.
We weren't sure about them, like monsters,
dangerous and likable at the same time.
(But we knew that they were not infallible-
we'd heard about Sputnik and Bay of Pigs).
Our main weapon against them was derision:
Sea Hunt (Lloyd Bridges parting seaweed)
Highway Patrol (Broderick Crawford
climbing painfiully out of his patrol car),
Jet Jackson, Davy Crockett. Sky King,
sent us into fits of laughter and parody.
But derision did not always work: westerns
were harder because the heroes were guys
like Steve McQueen in *Wanted Dead or Alive*
Chuck Connor (the razor jaw) *The Rifleman*,

Skidmark Calligraphy

Clint Eastwood in *Rawhide*, Richard Boone
as smooth Paladin in *Have Gun Will Travel.*
Against men as cool and merciless as these
we knew we probably didn't stand a chance.

Past Wars

I

For a peaceful small town there was a lot of war,
mostly under the long shadow of WWII
that hung over us the way Waterloo
must have hung over the Victorians.

'Bombs on Tokyo!' we'd yell, jumping down
like the bombardiers over Tokyo yelling
"Geronimo!" as they let go their payloads,
(100,000 civilians in a single night).

They were calling the name of the great
Chiricahua general who led his people
in resistance to the United States of America
in the Apache Wars only 60 years before.

II
An elderly bachelor who lived on Division Street
had been a sergeant in the British army,
Like a minor character out of Kipling,
and fought in many of the empire's wars:
Boer War, Boxer Rebellion, Northwest Rebellion,
Gallipoli, Iraq, the Irish Uprising, Sudan.
When he died they had lawn sale, a dream-like

Skidmark Calligraphy

collection of objects from distant worlds
spread out on the grass: sabres, flags,
lances, pith helmets, rugs, cushions, samovars
I managed to get a shillelagh with a lead core
and I never once stopped to consider
how many skulls it had actually cracked.

III
What did those words mean? *Ortona
Dieppe, the Scheldt Estuary,
Caen, Falaise Gap?* What
secrets did these foreign places hold?
The ribbons and scars of our fathers
and uncles meant little to us, seldom
spoken of except in the distance,
their long shadows hanging over:
the drone of an air raid siren,
buried far away, yet always present.
The absent-minded fingers
tapping out of Morse code
messages at the dinner table

The Last Horse

It should have been forty years earlier
that horse-drawn milk wagons
were on their way out but there it was,
as though transported from another age
onto our street for one last run.
We were sent out with sugar cubes
to feed the horse, the last horse,
somehow sensing the sense of occasion,
like Elvis coming to the Gardens
in Toronto, or a visit by the Queen.

As a child you are not small
to yourself, and your world is larger
than it ever will be again, but I felt small
beside that horse as it stood in our street
unblinking eyes behind leather blinders,
huge neck, curled back
lips, so soft on my little palm.
So long ago and yet so clear
in the late light of that afternoon
standing together, horse and boy,
in the heavy shadow of things gone by.

The Duke of Earl

The year is 1962.
The place is Lake Baptiste
up in the Kawarthas.
Four twelve-year old
boys are paddling and singing
Duke of Earl to the rhythm
of their strokes, exhausted
tiny voices on the lake.
They have been told
they are going to David Milne's
cabin, the famous painter.
When they get there it's a ruin,
half-filled with porcupine shit.
Years later, at a show
of Milne's prints, I am drawn
not to the prints but to the plates
gouged and scored across
So they can't be repeated,
and every time I see one
of those finely etched landscapes
I remember, not the waves,
or the sunlight or the voices,
or all the lost memories,
but Gene Chandler's voice,
the way it soars above.

Another Day

An ordinary day:
as usual we filed back
into school after recess,
boys through the boys door,
girls through the girls door,
jostling and fooling around,
but not so much as to attract
the attention of the duty teacher
who might send you to the Office,
where you could get the strap.
But there were no duty teachers-
they were all standing together
huddled at the top of the stairs,
 and some of them were crying.
I remember thinking: what
thing could have happened
that would make the teachers cry.

Bad Songs

It was the Year of the Terrible Songs.
Chuck Berry was in jail, Elvis in the army,
Little Richard had joined the church.
What we got was the worst of the worst.

Itsy bitsy teeny weeny yellow polkadot bikini
One-eyed three-horned flying purple people eater,
Oo-ee-oo-ah-ah I asked the witch doctor
Oo ee oo ah ah ting tang walla walla bing bang
Who put the bomp in the bompshu omp shu omp

Everyone knew how terrible it all was,
so terrible that it even made
Chubby Checker sound good.

But in amongst them there were some gems:
The Shirelles, early Miracles, the Marvelettes

And what we didn't know was
what they were getting us ready for:

The opening chords and then the words
that would change everything forever:

Oh yeah,

I'll

tell you something

I hope you'll understand.

The Shoop Shoop Song

A car backfires in the parking lot
faking a gunshot, and a flicker

Crosses the Tim Horton's, riding radio
waves that hold some simulacra

Of Betty Everett's voice, at once both
perfect and temporary, maintaining

It's in his kiss with some authority,
in fact insisting on it. *Is it in his eyes?*

Oh no, you'll be deceived. Is it in his sighs?
He'll make believe. (The instrumental

Break, a weirdly detached marimba solo)
Is it in his face? No, no that's just his charm

In his warm embrace? No, that's just his arm.
Meanwhile, at my table I'm trying to make

A little sanctuary inside it all,
made out of a coffee, a newspaper

And someone's collected poems. The world
presses in and I can't press back.

She's singing about what's real, what's
in his kiss and everything I need

to know about being in love suddenly
is there—b*ang!*—it becomes clear

That the kiss Betty Everett's singing about
is *my* kiss: it was *my* kiss that it was in

Skidmark Calligraphy

From *I Step Into a World*

Skidmark Calligraphy

I step into a world
equal parts magic
and devastation.
I wander off down
a path unforeseen.
Tankers, pipelines, sure
verities of need,
mixed with an old light
breaking through cedars
too tall to photograph,
totem poles too tall
to photograph. I know
that I know nothing.
Ravens' guttural
ask and answer.
I walk on your land.

He wanted some way of showing people things that were in his mind, things about the creatures and about himself and their relation to each other. He cut forms to fit the thoughts that the birds and animals and fish suggested to him, and to these he added something of himself. When they were all linked together they made very strong talk for the people. He grafted this new language onto the great cedar trunks and called them totem poles and stuck them up in the villages with great ceremony. Then the cedar and the creatures and the man all talked together through the totem poles to the people. The carver did even more—he let his imaginings rise above the objects that he saw and pictured supernatural beings too.

Emily Carr *Klee Wyck*, 'Greenville'

The Ocean View Hotel,
another glass of tequila.

The curtain flaps
open and closed.

On waves ranging
in ten thousand wrinkles,

Every one hand-picked
by the late sun's slant.

Entering deep in the mountains is
                    not avoiding the world,
only the desire to be far from floating fame.

Streams and stones, so blue-green,
Mists and evening clouds let go emotions.

Deep swimming fish don't take the bait,
Some forest birds have never been startled.

Surely I will dream of dissolving all dust,
Losing thoughts of an official career.

Shen Shichong, Ming Dynasty Painter-poet

Skidmark Calligraphy

Not many cities were founded by just one person, the way Thebes was founded by Cadmus. Prince Rupert was one of these. Charles M. Hays, President of the Pacific Grand Truck Railway, picked this place and put the town here, just like that. It was to be the Pacific end point of his railroad, based purely on questions of real estate value. Two other sites, Kitimat and Port Simpson, were more obvious and practical choices, but were rife with land speculation, so Hays bought the much less likely Prince Rupert site himself, paid something to the adjacent Tsimshian community, Metlakatla, and negotiated the sale with the Province of British Columbia. Hays' dream of a second transcontinental railroad, with Prince Rupert as its major Pacific terminal port city, ended when he drowned in the sinking of SS Titanic.

Not being from here
I couldn't say whether

It's a common occurrence
when a raven gets hit

By a car on the main street.
I only know I felt

A shudder in the mountains.

Prince Rupert is the North American port closest
to Shanghai
West Lake in Hangzhou was
          capital of the Southern Song

The tanker *Pearl of the Orient* moored at the bow,
          turns
Slowly In the fine rain like the dial of a compass

Banished to West Lake, Su Shi wrote

Drinking on West Lake, Clear Weather Followed By
Rain

Glistening sunlight on the water,
          best when the sky is clear,

Mountains shrouded in mist,
          rain has a charm of its own.

Skidmark Calligraphy

What one sees in the harbor is the concrete movement of goods. This movement can be explained in its totality only through recourse to abstraction.

Alan Sekula
Fish Story

Look sideways and it's a mountain,
look up and it's a peak.

Near, far, flying, crouching-
it will never stay the same.

And you can never know
the true face of Mount Hays

As long as you are standing
in the middle of the mountain.

Vietnamese Crabbers

i)

Vietnamese crabbers
in the Tim Horton's
fill the air
with sweet and sour
syllables and subtle
pungent melodies.
Vietnamese
has seven tones:
level, mid-level
haranguing high,
rising, sharp
mid-dropping,
tumbling high,
breaking rising,
and heavy low.
As I drink my coffee
I imagine the poetry,
not as words, but
as hallucinogenic
flowers floating
upwards from
open mouths.
To be a poet is
to hum with the wind
to ride the moon

Skidmark Calligraphy

and dream and
roam with clouds

From 'Feeling and Emotions',
Xuân Diêu (1917-1985)

ii)

One day I see four deer,
walking through town,

cross at the crosswalk
so orderly, keeping

Well between the lines.
A Vietnamese fisherman

Stops his pick-up
to look, and comments:

"They always do that:
they are better than the people."

In August 1910 Prime Minister Wilfred Laurier and his wife visited the new town of Prince Rupert. He was greeted by seven Chiefs. The leading Tsimshian chief, Chief Charles Dudoward of the Nisga'a, was called upon to give the speech on behalf of neighbouring First Nations. His speech was also carved into a paddle, which was presented to Laurier as a gift.

His speech began,

> *The Chiefs and People of the Nass, Bella Coola and Babine Indians Territories unite with our White Brethren to give you a glad welcome to this Northern Country.*

In addition a chief from the Haida spoke. This was Chief Charles Edenshaw, who, as well as being a hereditary clan chief, was the greatest Haida artist of his generation—many would say, of any culture and any generation. He presented Lady Laurier with a silver bracelet, which he had probably made himself.

Laurier also made a speech, which, although was not delivered in writing, was long remembered in the region. The *Prince Rupert Journal* reported his words:

> *To the countrymen of the aboriginal races he said he was pleased to hear from them. He wanted them to understand that the*

government would ever protect them. The
word of the Crown was sacred and the rights,
which they held would ever be maintained.

The Fairview terminal, which opened in 2007, is a
main export point for forest products, particularly
from northern B.C., destined for Shanghai, Hong Kong
and the South Korean city of Busan.

Products coming in through the terminal from Asia
include apparel, consumer electronics, auto parts and
building materials, which are carried mainly by rail
throughout North America.

Prince Rupert's port is the second largest on
Canada's West Coast and the closest North American
port to Asia.

Globe and Mail Report on Business
March 10, 2015

The mighty turbines of a world economy
go roaring past Prince Rupert

Meanwhile in town, from hand to hand,

There is exchange
of a yogurt container of
Salmonberry
or *Rubus Spectabilis*
or *ma̱gooxs*
for a bucket of
Dungeness crab
(or *Metacarcinus magister*
or *ga̱lmoos)*
for a bag of
pine or Matsutake
mushrooms
(or*Tricholoma matsutake*
or *gaayda baa'lax)*
for a jar of
black gooseberries
(or *Ribes divaricatum*
or *dales*
for a can of
   smoked sockeye
   (or *Oncorhynchus nerka*
   or *miso)*
for a mess of
   blackberries

Skidmark Calligraphy

(or *Rubus allegheniensis)*
for a tin of
  chocolate chip cookies
  (or *Crustulum socolatius)*
for a bottle of
  homemade lager
  (or *cervisia).*

An economy made
apparently for
  and by human beings
  (or *homo sapiens)*
  (or *gigyet).*

...the sea remains the crucial space of globalization.
Nowhere else is the disorientation, violence, and
alienation of contemporary capitalism more manifest,
but this truth is not self-evident, and must be
approached as a puzzle, or mystery, a problem to be
solved.

Allan Sekula & Noël Burch
Notes for a Film

Your boat shuttles through the mist
on the way to Dodge Cove.

Cloudy mountains appear and
disappear. The mind follows

High mountain trails, the inlet
returns like a remembered thought.

Skidmark Calligraphy

The cargo container, a standardized metal box, capable of being quickly transferred from ship to highway lorry to railroad train, has radically transformed the space and time of port cities and ocean passages.

The boxes are everywhere, mobile and anonymous, their contents hidden from view. One could say that these containers are "coffins of remote labor-power" carrying goods manufactured somewhere else, by invisible workers on the other side of the globe. We are told by the apologists of globalization that this accelerated flow is indispensable for our continued prosperity and for the deferred future prosperity of those who labor so far away. But perhaps, this is a case for Pandora, or for her more clairvoyant sister, Cassandra.

Alan Sekula & Noël Burch
Notes on The Forgotten Space

Millions of containers
pass by Dodge Cove,

Spanish galleons
loaded down with gold.

There are no cars here
so we walk,

Pass a guy
nailing shingles

'Need any help?'

Skidmark Calligraphy

The international energy company Nexen Energy has
picked Digby Island for a proposed $20 billion LNG
terminal with the goal of shipping 10 to 20 million
tons of LNG from B.C. to Asia each year.

CBC News, Dec 2, 2014

Dodge Cove

now has a grizzly,
some say two.

It is the first
siting here-
driven down

To the coast
by logging
mines and pipelines-

Already the stuff
of local legends
and bad jokes.

It becomes a story
although in our hearts
we know there is fear.

[Salmon Run, Skidegate]

What salmon know
is a place
embedded in
salmon.

Neither knower
nor known.

We know they are talking
to each other but we don't know
what they are sayin'

Here they are throwing
their emaciated bodies

over the gravel,

Offering death to life.
I stand on the bridge
and think of Zhuangzi

And the happiness of fish.

Skidmark Calligraphy

A curtain of drizzle lifts on the Skeena.
Red sun painting the mountainsides

Scatters diamonds the length of the river.
Mountains shear straight into the water.

Listen for something as though laying your ear
on a steel rail: silence.

Skeena dawn Skeena dusk:
I can't tell them apart in memory.

A day happened in between,
then disappeared, lost to me forever.

Gullies and ridges still unvisited
carpets of wildflowers still unnamed

Emerald moss fills every path
Fog soaks right through to the skin

So far from home,
I wander on my way to nowhere

All at once the sun
puts in a brief appearance,

breaking up the shadows.

In a place of rain and mist
people pay close attention to sunlight.

I seems like I just arrived here
and it's already time to leave.

Skidmark Calligraphy

Since it's already dark by four,
I go for an early supper:

Bowl of phô, couple of beers
then out into the street

To find spread across the sky—
Boom!—the Northern Lights!

Back in my little hotel room
I lie in bed dreaming of home.

Arthur Bull

From *One Hundred Sonnets*

Skidmark Calligraphy

We think we know what we need to know, but what
we need to know is always a lot more interesting
than what we think, and what we're never knowing
about ourselves is more than enough to fill the lot.
So, what we need to be thinking really ought
to be not about how we need to know if this thing
or that is what we need, but that it brings
us back to our needing to think about what brought
this need to think about our needs at all,
especially the need to know about ourselves
which seems such a natural need at first,
until we know the way it makes us fall
backwards and down the never ending hall
of mirrors reflecting needs. Then it gets worse.

We're multifaceted and that's a fact
we easily forget. Like diamonds, the value
is more the more facets they have. That's due
to the light and sparkle as they refract.
We forget this with people when we act
as though they had just one or very few,
reducing them the way we often do
to a flat cartoon of who they are that lacks
all depth, or worse, a blank screen onto which
we project our needs, and insecurities,
impulses, assumptions and even spite.
Enough of that. We can't afford that much
loss of ourselves and our humanity,
or miss the beauty of that reflected light.

Skidmark Calligraphy

To live on the edge of collapsing empires is to know
your place. Our ploughs turn up muskets, ginger jars.
and skulls. News and disease are delivered from afar.
Aircraft carriers and slavers come and go
on the horizon. Slug, seagull, earwig and crow
are sovereign now. People in abandoned cars.
The Centre will tell us if we're at peace or war.
Distant hoof beats. The servants assemble in a row
to watch master and mistress open up their veins.
Charters proclaimed that we were always first.
The First World. The bringers of the best
of everything, but we always knew the game.
It was just the latest version of the worst,
and we will pay the price with all the rest.

Back in the woods a tin cup hangs on a tree
next to a pool that's fed by a little spring
put there to serve as ladle, a thoughtful thing.
Printed on the bottom almost too faint to see:
Made in Yugoslavia, and with these three
words, a faded coat of arms that brings
old echoes of ancient empires and their kings,
and sudden thoughts of distant unities
of church and state as old as Byzantine.
The two-headed eagle, and that nations fall
apart and disappear, and all the worse
politics prevail, and neighbours learn to hate.
I dip the orange cup into the cold stream
on this hot day and wonder how it can heal
a broken world, to cool that terrible heat.

This cotton shirt provides a map of suffering
that traces trade routes back to children's hands
in a Bangladeshi factory. High school bands
play a rousing Sousa march called King
Cotton, a hymn to the slave economy, a bigger thing
than all the other industries combined,
including railroads, the centrepost of the land.
In Gandhi's works the margin notes by King
mark that when India was under Britain's heel
it was cotton again that fed the empires maw,
this soft fabric that made the iron law
of exploitation, till the turning of Mahatma's wheel.
I put on the shirt increasingly aware
it is the weight of history we must wear.

How many times will I have to see the end
of the world? How many apocalypses more?
How any Armageddon's are still in store?
It's not that easy, something you can mend
over and over like darning socks. I'll send
my regrets next time. I've seen it all before.
The same skipping record of pestilence and war
keeps sending messages no one understands.
There's little doubt: today the world is burning
and yet it feels familiar somehow
and even if there is no single ray
of hope, perhaps that's why we should be turning
our minds to think on what is justice now,
even if it's the very last of days.

Skidmark Calligraphy

How can they be serious about the Rule of Law?
The countries that plundered the planet preach,
having destroyed whatever was in their reach,
bombing and invading, that's what the world saw
without the slightest pretense, except for raw
naked power and greed, no need for speech
when force will do the trick. They cannot teach
any country about legality. The gall,
hypocrisy and arrogance astound.
These principled thugs who will never earn
the right to speak down to the world from higher
ground now talk of reason and they love the sound
of their own virtuous voices, but we have learned
to never trust the words of thieves and liars.

It's such a joke to say that what is good
is my own true nature beneath this mess
of shallow thoughtless contradictoriness,
For this I blame the modals: should and could
and worst of all, my own worst enemy, would.
An answer that is never no or yes,
a parallel universe of infinite regress,
and verbs forever in subjunctive mood.
Even walking through the heavenly hills,
I'd be wrapped up in a vague quandariness
preserving a private purgatory there.
Somehow lacking even a lack of will,
I'd drift in a sea of possibility, unless
of course, I chanced to meet a grizzly bear.

[On His Blandness]
It's not a complement to say 'It's bland'.
In fact it might be worse than just plain 'bad'.
Something watered down and weak that had
little conviction and never took a stand.
But there is another way to understand
that even-tempered sensibility, instead
look to the mild aesthetic, which the Chinese said
was highest, as in West Lake's temperate scan.
But these calm pleasures definitely are not
for everyone: it's not a Vegas show,
not for peaking on Sublime, or rattling nerves
and not for those who like their yoga hot,
not for the impatient, and certainly also
those who can't stand to wait to be served.

To make a mistake is not at all the same
as making a birdhouse, a fuss or making do.
Experience will attest (and I've made a few)
it's something else. When avoiding blame
we say 'I'm sorry, I was mistaken' the main
emphasis is on my error. But the shoe
is on the other foot with accident, when you
say it was the fault of fate (or so you claim).
To have an accident is not the same as to have
a headache. If I sunk your boat by accident
it means my cannon had misfired (too bad).
If I sunk it by mistake it means that I had meant
to sink the boat beside it. But maybe this is moot:
The outcome is the same: there is a sunken boat.

Skidmark Calligraphy

A Narrative is walking down the street.
She stops to take a look in a store window,
a smoke shop where, arranged in little rows,
a large collection of toy cars, very neat,
metal miniatures, obsessively complete.
She waits a bit and then decides to go
inside to buy a box of cigarillos
called Schimmelpenninck, her secret treat.
Walking on, she wonders about the cars
and also on what it really means to be
a Narrative, and whether it's just a joke.
Eventually she comes to a favourite bar,
where she meets an Example, one that she
slightly knows, and asks him "Do you smoke?"

I think hallucinations were the best
part of the Sixties, never mentioned much
by all those documentaries and such.
In those visionary moments we were blessed
with illuminated sights, wonderful and vast,
sounds you could see, colours you could touch,
cascades of flowers coming down, or watch
office buildings melt in waves and crests.
(I had a friend who saw the Faerie Queen
appear in his fireplace.) You might say.
'What use are these imaginary schemes,
that are not there and never truly seen?'
And I might say, 'What use is there anyway
of any beauty, even in a dream?'

142

There is only one world and it's no world at all.
There's only one sky, but it was never there.
There is no earth, no ocean nor any air,
nothing in fact and nothing you would call
real ever was, even the rise and fall
of galaxies absent their solar glare.
With nothing left we finally are aware
that even awareness's transparent wall
is gone, and still we have to ask what's left,
refusing the possibility of total loss
we grasp at straws, and anything will do
to stop how much we'd have to be bereft.
But all that disappearing now seems soft
compared to the hard fact of losing you.

Then, having given up on sleep, I rose
and went to search the bookshelves for your poems
or anything really- letters, old unknown
articles, lost prose pieces, reviews of shows.
It was your voice I craved, the way you chose
your words, a quiet questioning tone
a style that was always yours and yours alone.
it was all of this but what I missed the most
was something you wrote, the way that it was said,
a word of hope in a world that hope had left.
At last, conceding the book was likely lost,
I gave up, defeated, and went back to bed
without your voice I felt my way, bereft.

Skidmark Calligraphy

Outside, black branches move against the grey.
Inside, a power-out, it's darker still.
High winds have downed a line, and imposed a will
to withhold energy, making a night of day.
We were always very well-prepared the way
that only worriers can be: lamps to fill
with kerosene, candles set on window sills,
batteries charged, each source of light arrayed.
Abandoned by the big world we would make
a little refuge of our darkened home
filled with a floating galaxy, all flicker and glow.
Suddenly the lights come on, the house awakes
to the knowledge that, lit up, it's all alone,
and I realize I prefer the darkness now.

Do you remember those dams we used to build
on the little rivers that ran between the wide
expanse of sandbars at the Bay's low tide?
We were engineers of hydrodynamics, highly-skilled
in crisis management, working hard until
the ocean returned and, on every side,
the edifice that we'd built with so much pride—
        channels,
ponds, sluice gates, dams—was filled
with flood. It didn't bother us at all.
Today, as the broken world and all its mess
dissolves with every design in waves of doom
I want that energy and detachment, and to recall,
undistracted by hope or hopelessness,
the wide sandbars those sunny afternoons.

Arthur Bull

Skidmark Calligraphy

Skidmark Calligraphy

i) The Road

The buck lifted
out of the fog
into his windshield,
so the last thing
that they both saw
was each other.

Traffic stops for
road construction,
and all at once
the air fills up
with willow down
indicating
the change in speed.

A conversation between
a charm bracelet
and the pink granite
boulders in the woods
beside the highway.

Saturday night!
Two ponytails
in a Chevy pick-up.

Skidmark Calligraphy

Going back
to my place,
the big boom
SUV
DJ thump
I was hearing
was my heart.

The drop of rain,
after crawling
upward for such
a long, long time,
now finally
laid its burden
down on my hood.

On the way there,
the river was
fulltide brimming.
On the way back,
it was no more
than a trickle,
empty except for
one clam digger.

Driving away
from the sunset,
my rearview
mirror goes gold.

A conversation
between a dark road
and a lit-up ballgame.

Those skidmarks make
a delicate
calligraphy
out of last night's
burning rubber.

ii) Back Dooryard

Last night, storm.
This morning,
the silence
of bamboo
wind chimes, each
one lying
separately
on the grass.

The orange butterfly
disappears, becoming
another touch-me-not.

A doe and a fawn
go lifting lightly
over the high ferns.

A breeze shakes down
yesterday's rain
from today's trees,
sweet and shy as
baby's rattle.

A student of Zeno,
the moth that had fallen
into the pail of water
paddled, first halfway across,
then halfway across again.

Winter's firewood
in 4 ft. lengths,
waiting to be
bucked, split and stacked
like yarrow stalks,
just now thrown down.

That Nor'easter
is going along
the very same
path the glacier
was going along.

Freya, Grey Goddess,
our dear cat, now gone,
investigating
the rainwater caught
in a storm window
left out on the lawn
gingerly dabbed
her right paw into
her own reflection.

Skidmark Calligraphy

Pouring from one
to the other,
I pondered pail
versus bucket.

Fresh snow falls
from a branch:
crows playing.

This rain barrel
once brimful of
dancing sunlight,
is now frozen
hard as steel and
glares back at me:
'*I'm* still sparkling'

A conversation
between a ginger jar
and a stand of rock maple.

After the ice storm
sunlight in the clearing
turned on the alders.

This foundation
is now home to
a family of
sapling maples.

The cross-section
of the old maple,
when I cut it,
showed how it had
grown out around
a spike driven
through all the rings,
each one a year,
year after year,
until it reached
deeply piercing
into heartwood.

Spring, a red
ribbon on
a wreath from
last Christmas,
uncovered.

My green tomatoes
are racing the frost.
They'll never know red
if the race is lost.

Rain's marimba patter
on forest bed leaves
flickers filtered sunlight.

Clang! The first
daffodil
opened up.

Skidmark Calligraphy

Tiny and fierce,
these hummingbirds
zip 'round the garden
at such high speed
it puts the rest
of the morning
in slow motion.

iii) History

Blomidon's
borrowed light.

This land
has laws.
Break them,
and you
will pay.

You ask on what
the sovereignty
of the state rests,
if not violence.

Sage smoke curling
upwards shapes words
that say never
forget, never
ever, forget.

Skidmark Calligraphy

My grandmother's
five-year-old hands,
blue from picking
wild blueberries,
on a hillside
a lot like this.
(1894)

Do not forget
that history
is as about
as purposeful
as a bayonet.

For me the smell
of chamomile
tea meant healthy.
For her it meant
the memory of
a war, cold trains
and labour camps,
muttering as
she left the room.

Is it primitive
accumulation
melting the glacier?

In between the event
and the story we made
of it there wasn't much
time, nor for that matter
was there very much space.

Snow geese rise above
Riviére Saint Laurent,
leaving what happened
there, as though startled
by a silent bell.

The two ambushes
that once happened here,
forty years apart,
must be why it's called
Bloody Creek, so named
because both times they
turned the water red.

History neither
flows backward nor
forward, but more
likely it goes in
and then goes out,
much like the tide.

iv) Signage

The sign says
BEWARE OF
FALLING ICE.

What to do?

Sign in store window:
EVERYTHING MUST GO,
as though we hadn't
guessed that already.

"Canadians" like
the seeming distance
quotation marks give.

Today I learned
some new vocab,
spelled out in
the white script of
old coyote scat.

The bear wanting in
to our cabin, left
calligraphy-like
claw marks on the wall
like a translation
of the Jia Dao poem:
"Sorry I missed you"

Is any eggplant
a commodity?
isn't the question.
The question is
When is an eggplant
a commodity?

You might be having
an *ah-ha* moment,
but bear I mind that
I might be having
a *ho-hum* moment.

When ideas happen,
what happens? What
is happening?

Skidmark Calligraphy

Spoke and rim
spoke and rim

Spoke and hub
Spoke and hub

Spoken word
Spoken word

Deer tracks inside
my snowshoe tracks-
for easier hopping
I would suppose-
are crisscrossed by
coyote tracks

v) Birds

I couldn't count
how many ways the
woodpecker could
divide the beat.

That high-note-triplet-low-note bird
sings of instability.

in the snowy maples. I make a mental note
to look it up

later, but the bird, lifting off, says *No, not later.*
Name me now.

Seagulls leaning
into the wind
might lend themselves
to poetry though
generally they
prefer pizza.

Skidmark Calligraphy

A murmuration
of starlings churn
and torque, their thickness
inflating the square
between office towers,
then loosen knotted
clouds of sixteenth notes
before they leave to
sleep under the bridge

No, geese can't be V-shaped
thoughts, any more than
ragged sentences, or I-shaped
concepts diagrammed
across the sky. No, what
is perfectly formed is not
there shape, but their direction.

Seven eider ducks
paddling are printed
on the still surface
along the lower edge
of the Bay's long scroll.

Pointing out
at the swell
on the bay,
did you say
Black Ducks or
was it black
ducks?

That Northern Gannet,
pierced
the bay's skin,
like a syringe.

vi) Shore

In the summer
heat
that scraggly
spruce
bears witness to winter.
its branches
pointing
all one direction.

Sleek and black
the mink flows
over basalt
the way lava
must have flowed.

That line on the water
could be a floating log
or a feeding whale
or a hyphen in-
between land and sea
or it could just be a line.

A damselfly
barely touches
the pool's surface,
and goes, before
the ripples go
over the face
of the blue sky.

A seagull
flies across
a tidepool.

Scarves of kelp
wave goodbye
to the out-
going tide.

Caught in between
basalt boulders,
a child's plastic
flip-flop, turquoise.

Skidmark Calligraphy

We know the ocean
yields up everything
and anything, but
what could have led to
this, a basketball
up in a spruce tree?

One man, one boat,
one line, six hooks,
attempting to
destroy the fishery.

vii) Short Novels

A conversation
between a hairclip
and a bed table.

The test results
came back the night
of the wedding party.

Working split shift
at SuperStore,
medicated,
sick on her feet:
'Have a nice day.'

They said you were flighty.
What would that mean, 'flighty'?
Something I will never
know, now that you have flown.

Skidmark Calligraphy

Amid
rising
voices,
Dragon
Well leaves
slowly
sink in
your glass.

Your voicemail left
its mark on me
like a tattoo,
indelible.

The guttering candle.
lets daybreak flutter down
from its perch to its roost.

Athena enters
in pink slacks and yellow
rainboots: she is
all attitude.

I bought a ticket
thinking the play had
an ensemble cast
but as it turned out
it was a one-man show.

      A drunken man

tries to por

               -tage

        a ca

                  -noe

The sign by the tracks
said NO TRAIN WHISTLE,
killing many songs.

I can sympathize with Ovid.
His exile was a living hell.
After only months of COVID
I am yearning for Rome as well.

Skidmark Calligraphy

Just when you think
you have a handle
on the future,
a Portuguese
marching band comes
around the corner.

She knew
I was a sailor
by the way
I wore my pants.

Something smelled bad
but nobody
wanted to look
under the porch.

So what's the worst
thing could happen?
You could die. So
what, I said, I
could live with that

Airports need
high ceilings
for the strong
emotions.

Equality without difference
is bad equality.
Difference without equality
is bad difference.

I am broken
open. Now you
can come in.

Skidmark Calligraphy

Four Fourteeners

I
I had just returned from a long trip and,
        for some reason,
I needed something from the stationery drawer,
        I forget what.

This is one of those old wooden drawers
        that is built into the wall.
When I opened it a huge squirrel
        leaped out at me.

Now 'huge' might not seem like a good adjective
        for a squirrel, but when it
is coming out of a drawer in your house,
        it might as well be four feet long.

It had apparently gnawed a little entrance
        in the back of the drawer
and made a sizable nest there
        out of chewed-up foam rubber.

I try to see it from the squirrel's point of view,
        in its nest there,
the safest possible place in the world,
        and imagine what it would be like for

Me, sleeping in my cozy bed,
  being awakened by the sight of the roof
being lifted off and seeing
  the Cyclops staring down at me.

It was an emotional experience, for the both of us.
  I grabbed a poker
and started chasing to around the house,
  all the while yelling

'You stupid fuck, what are doing in my house,
  you get the fuck out'
through living room, kitchen
  and finally into the wood cupboard.

I should say that the poker
  was not intended to be used to kill it,
but rather as a defensive weapon
  in case the creature turned on me.

I have heard people whose houses
  have been burgled say how they felt violated
but having a wild animal in your house
  takes that to a deeper primordial level.

It hid behind the woodpile,
  and I retreated to the sofa to re-group,
exhausted and confused. Apparently,
  the squirrel sneaked out the open door.

Skidmark Calligraphy

It took me a long time to recover—
       I assume it was the same for the squirrel—
and now it has this dramatic story to tell
       family and friends, and I have this poem

II

This story starts when I was travelling in Java where
I had a nasty fall down some slippery stone stairs.

I didn't break any bones, amazingly,
       only cuts and scrapes
I patched them up and went on,
       happy about my escape

From serious injury. Fast forward to
       three days later on
in Ubud on a sunny afternoon,
       I was walking toward town,

When, looking down, I noticed that
       the underside of my left arm
had turned a bright, brilliant green,
       much to my alarm.

This could only point to one thing,
       I quickly realized: gangrene
from the wounds, and immediately saw
       what that could mean

My thoughts raced to everything I knew about it,
        and the implication:
what usually results from this
        is immediate amputation.

I kept on walking in hopes of finding
        a hospital or pharmacy
and tried to reconcile myself to
        what fate had in store for me.

A one-armed guitarist—
        I had to stop and touch my heart.
No one had ever done such a thing,
        not even Django Reinhardt.

I'd have to learn new ways to play,
        to somehow drum and thump
People would say, "It's amazing what he can do
        with just a stump."

My thoughts turned to possible
        and long-awaited celebrity
on You Tube, maybe even
        my own show of reality TV.

I thought of all the sympathy, arriving home,
        and all the warm
(half) embraces I'd receive because I'd lost my arm.

Skidmark Calligraphy

I finally found a pharmacy
        and presented my tragedy.
The pharmacist looked at it,
        and then looked hard at me.

Finally she said 'bruise', paused and smiled
        then said 'bruise cream'.
It was a relief even though
        it meant losing my tragic dreams.

All my plans and consolations disappeared
        as I applied the ointment
gladly exchanging my left arm for
        that little disappointment.

III

The first job that I ever had was at the CNE
it was many, many years ago,
        but its left its mark on me.

I was only 15, happy to have a summer wage.
I was supposed to be 18, but I lied about my age.

I was a security guard, I thought it might be fun
I got to wear a uniform and they offered me a gun.

(I decided against the pistol,
      after giving it some thought
imagining a shootout on the Midway,
      and maybe getting shot).

Having declined the sidearm,
      Smith & Wesson if I recall
they took me to the lower basement
      of Old Toronto City Hall

Where I had to swear an oath
      on an old volume that looked
a lot like a worn-out copy
      of a Methodist prayer book.

Suited up in my beige uniform,
      police hat and Sam Brown,
they took me to my guard post
      at the Exhibition Grounds.

There was a huge drum where I was
      supposed to stand
with a big sign that said
      Win a Trip to Disneyland.

Apparently delinquent kids
      were stuffing sticks and gum
and even firecrackers in
      the little slot on the drum

Skidmark Calligraphy

Where contestants were supposed to put
     their filled-in entries
for their chance for Disneyland,
     hence the need of a sentry.

A boring job, but there were some perks,
     one for example:
I was near the Pure Foods Building
     and got a lot of free samples

(On the sign "Pure Foods"
     was highlighted in quotation
marks, a late example of Old Canadian punctuation.)

Plus, there were the rides, as many as I could take
at half-price, between reading
     Rimbaud on my breaks.

The worst part was the barker
     right opposite the drum
at the toss game with stuffed animals
     for the few who ever won.

All day, without a break he yelled
     the very same refrain
'Doggy-doggy, doggy-doggy' driving
     both of us insane.

On bad nights it still comes to me,
      a nightmare that I have
I fear the doggy-doggy chant
      will haunt me to my grave.

They say putting on a uniform
      divides the boys from men
Don't know about that, but I can say,
      I never put one on again.

IV

After I had my eye exam, they said I needed glasses.
The kind that they prescribed
      had lenses call progressives.

When you look down, they go close up and change
when you look up they go to longer range.

They follow your eyes the way a shadow might
except that shadows can only follow light

and eyes have a quite different relationship with it
not exactly taking it in but somehow
      seeing through it

in which the light goes into them
      (at least that's how it's seeming)
to create these inner shadows
      of vision with its beaming.

Skidmark Calligraphy

Perhaps it is more like photosynthesis
the way vegetables eat light in order to exist.

Our personalities are a lot like shadows too,
only visible when we are awake
        with many things to do,

or alive or conscious because apparently
        when we're dead,
asleep or unconscious we don't have one,
        or so it's said.

because there is nowhere to cast
        that shadow in the mind.
And when I say 'cast', I don't mean t
        he trout fishing kind,

or the hard wrapping you get when
        you break a bone,
or the actors in a play, or your cast of mind
        when you're alone,

but more like the direction where you
        cast your eyes—
up or down, and near or far,
        they go progressive-wise.

'Nothing to do with politics', I said,
        and we both laughed,
'since those progressives generally
        are only looking left.'

Arthur Bull

Skidmark Calligraphy

Acknowledgements

I have been very fortunate in the various publishers and presses that have put out my work over the years. I want to take this opportunity to thank them all, including some who are no longer with us, for their generous support and encouragement. It is hard to exaggerate how important this has been to me in my life as a writer. They are:

> Joe Blades (Broken Jaw Press)
> Kathleen Tudor (Roseway Publishing)
> Bev Daurio (teksteditions)
> Richard Grove (Hidden Brook Press)
> Bill Ripley (Another New Calligraphy)
> Vincent Ponka (Emmerson Street Press)
> David Zieroth (Alfred Gustav Press)
> Anna Faktorovich (Anaphora Literary Press)
> Andrew Wetmore
>   (Moose House Publications)

I like to imagine this wonderfully interesting group of people sitting around a table in a pub, and the conversations they might be having. On that occasion I would raise a glass to all of them to express my heartfelt gratitude.

Skidmark Calligraphy

About the author

Arthur Bull lives in Lake Midway on Digby Neck, in Nova Scotia. He has published seven books of poetry and five chap-books, and his poems and translations from classical Chinese have appeared in numerous Canadian, US and inter-national journals. He is also a musician and has  been part of the improvised music scene in Canada for more than 40 years.

As a long-time activist he has worked primarily with small-scale fisheries organizations and rural development organizations at the local, national and international level.